BUILDING THE
PANAMA CANAL

KELLY DOUDNA

Consulting Editor, Diane Craig, M.A./Reading Specialist

Super Sandcastle

An Imprint of Abdo Publishing
abdopublishing.com

abdopublishing.com

Published by Abdo Publishing, a division of ABDO, PO Box 398166, Minneapolis, Minnesota 55439. Copyright © 2018 by Abdo Consulting Group, Inc. International copyrights reserved in all countries. No part of this book may be reproduced in any form without written permission from the publisher. Super SandCastle™ is a trademark and logo of Abdo Publishing.

Printed in the United States of America, North Mankato, Minnesota
062017
092017

THIS BOOK CONTAINS RECYCLED MATERIALS

Editor: Lauren Kukla
Content Developer: Mighty Media, Inc.
Cover and Interior Design and Production: Mighty Media, Inc.
Photo Credits: iStockphoto; Library of Congress; Mighty Media, Inc.; National Archives and Records Administration; Shutterstock; Wikimedia Commons

Publisher's Cataloging-in-Publication Data

Names: Doudna, Kelly, author.
Title: Building the Panama Canal / by Kelly Doudna.
Description: Minneapolis, MN : Abdo Publishing, 2018. | Series: Engineering marvels.
Identifiers: LCCN 2016962890 | ISBN 9781532111136 (lib. bdg.) | ISBN 9781680788983 (ebook)
Subjects: LCSH: Panama Canal--Panama--Juvenile literature. | Canals--Design and construction--Juvenile literature. | Hydraulic engineering--Juvenile literature.
Classification: DDC 627--dc23
LC record available at http://lccn.loc.gov/2016962890

Super SandCastle™ books are created by a team of professional educators, reading specialists, and content developers around five essential components—phonemic awareness, phonics, vocabulary, text comprehension, and fluency—to assist young readers as they develop reading skills and strategies and increase their general knowledge. All books are written, reviewed, and leveled for guided reading, early reading intervention, and Accelerated Reader™ programs for use in shared, guided, and independent reading and writing activities to support a balanced approach to literacy instruction.

CONTENTS

WHAT IS A CANAL?

A canal is a water channel. People build canals. Ships travel through them. The Panama Canal is famous. It connects two oceans. They are the Atlantic and the Pacific. This canal makes it easier to ship goods around the world.

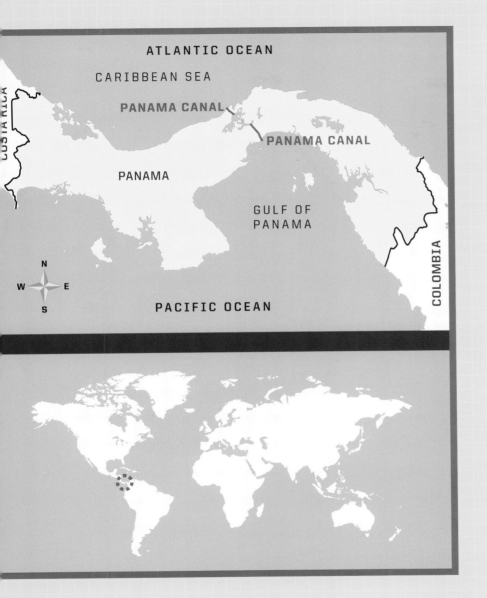

THE PANAMA CANAL

LOCATION: Panama

BUILDING STARTED:
June 28, 1904

BUILDING COMPLETED:
August 15, 1914

CHIEF ENGINEERS:

- John Findlay Wallace (chief engineer from 1904 to 1905)
- John Frank Stevens (chief engineer from 1905 to 1907)
- George Washington Goethals (chief engineer from 1907 to 1914)

LENGTH: 50 miles (80 km)

A LONG TRIP

People have used ships to move goods for a long time. But it was not always as easy as it is today. Ships could not quickly cross between the Pacific and the Atlantic. They had to sail around South America. People thought about building a canal as early as the 1500s. It would connect the two oceans. The canal would cut across Panama. French workers tried to build such a canal in the 1800s. But they failed.

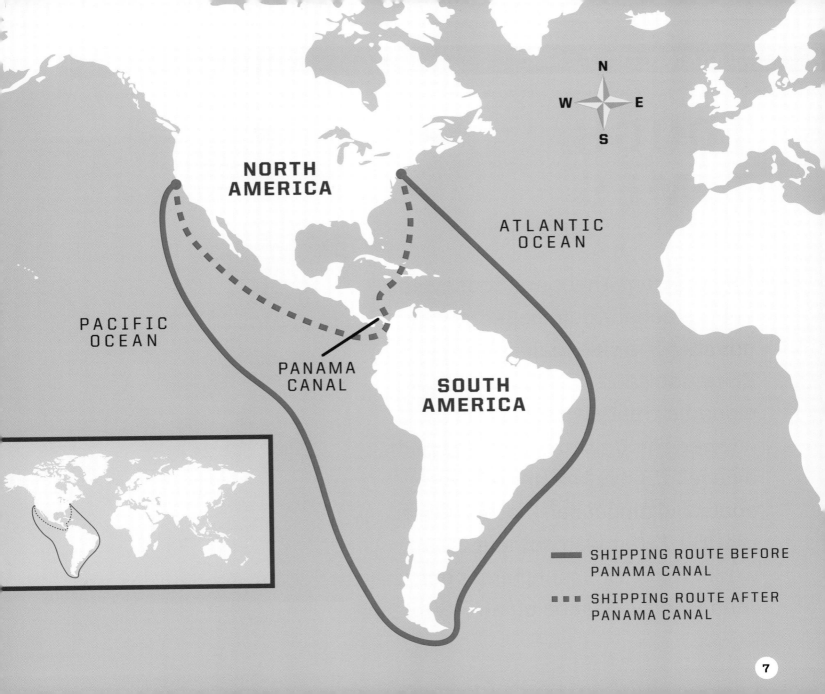

NORTH
AMERICA

ATLANTIC
OCEAN

PACIFIC
OCEAN

PANAMA
CANAL

SOUTH
AMERICA

SHIPPING ROUTE BEFORE
PANAMA CANAL

SHIPPING ROUTE AFTER
PANAMA CANAL

TOUGH TIMES

US president Theodore Roosevelt knew a canal would help his country. It would make shipping US goods easier. In 1903, he signed a treaty with Panama. It allowed the United States to build a canal. It gave the United States control of the canal. Digging began in 1904. But it was not easy. Many workers got sick. Chief Engineer John Findlay Wallace quit in 1905.

President Theodore Roosevelt

The Panama Canal route went through thick jungle and tall mountains.

A NEW PLAN

A lock on the Panama Canal

Roosevelt did not give up. He hired John Frank Stevens to take over the project. Stevens made the canal's **design** better. Wallace's plan called for a **sea level** canal. But this canal was hard to dig. Stevens made a new plan. It used **locks** and dams. They would raise ships up above sea level. Workers did not need to dig as deep.

President Roosevelt visited workers at the Panama Canal in 1906.

DIGGING

George Washington Goethals took over as chief engineer in 1907. He split the work into three parts. One group started on the Atlantic side. Another worked on the Pacific side. A third group worked in the middle. They cut through a mountain range. **Dikes** were built at the canal's ends. They kept water out.

Workers dug a passage through the mountains in 1912. It was known as the Culebra Cut.

George Washington Goethals

GEORGE WASHINGTON GOETHALS

BORN: 1858, New York City

DIED: 1928, New York City

George Washington Goethals was in the US military. He was also an engineer. He had worked on other canals and **locks**. Goethals was a strong leader. He closely watched the building of the Panama Canal. He made sure workers used the best tools. He improved working conditions. The canal was done two years early!

JOINING OCEANS

Steam shovels did much of the digging. Meanwhile, workers built six concrete **locks**. Two steam shovels met in the canal's center in 1913. US president Woodrow Wilson blew up the last **dike** soon after. The canal filled with water. The two oceans were joined! The canal opened to ships in 1914.

Water rushes through the canal after the dike is blown up.

The SS Ancon was one of the first ships to travel through the canal.

NOT BIG ENOUGH

The Panama Canal was only 50 miles (80 km) long. But it saved ships more than 8,000 miles (13,000 km)! Many ships used the canal. But soon some ships were too big to do so. Panama gained control of the canal in 1999. The country's leaders knew something had to be done. They decided to **expand** the canal.

In 1977 US president Jimmy Carter (left) made an agreement with Panama. It said the country would gain control of the canal in 1999.

Many modern cruise ships are too big to fit through the original canal.

SUPER SHIPPING

Workers began improving the canal in 2007. They added new **locks**. They made the canal wider. They also made it deeper. The new canal opened in 2016.

The Panama Canal has helped shipping around the world. It makes it cheaper to move goods. This helps global trade. **Cruise ships** also use the canal to move people. This makes travel easier. The Panama Canal is an engineering marvel!

Panama Canal construction, 2016

CANALS
OF THE WORLD

GRAND CANAL
LOCATION: China

FIRST SEGMENT BUILT: 468 BCE

FINAL SEGMENT BUILT: 1368 CE

LENGTH: 1,100 miles (1,770 km)

BENEFITS: connects the cities of Beijing and Hangzhou

VENICE CANALS
LOCATION: Italy

FIRST BUILT: about 400 CE

SYSTEM LENGTH: 26 miles (42 km)

BENEFITS: more than 200 canals connect 118 islands that form the city of Venice

The Panama Canal is just one of many awesome canals. Check out these other cool canals!

ERIE CANAL

LOCATION: New York, United States

BUILT: 1825

LENGTH: 363 miles (584 km)

BENEFITS: connects the Great Lakes and New York City using the Hudson River

SUEZ CANAL

LOCATION: Egypt

BUILT: 1869

LENGTH: 120 miles (193 km)

BENEFITS: connects the Mediterranean Sea and the Red Sea

MORE ABOUT
THE PANAMA CANAL

More than **75,000 WORKERS** built the Panama Canal.

As many as **40 SHIPS** use the canal each day.

A ship takes about **TEN HOURS** to travel through the Panama Canal.

TEST YOUR KNOWLEDGE

1. Which US president signed a treaty with Panama in 1903 to build the Panama Canal?

2. The canal was built at **sea level**. TRUE OR FALSE?

3. In what year did the **expanded** Panama Canal open?

THINK ABOUT IT!

Is there a canal near where you live? How do you think it is used?

ANSWERS: 1. Theodore Roosevelt 2. False 3. 2016

GLOSSARY

cruise ship – a ship that carries passengers traveling for fun and stops at different ports.

design – to plan how something will appear or work.

dike – a wall or dam that is built to hold back water.

expand – to make or become larger.

lock – a part of a canal with gates in which boats can be lowered or raised by changing the water level.

sea level – the average height of the surface of the ocean.